WOMAN'S CHANGE OF LIFE

Vital facts on all aspects of the menopause, including
advice for reducing the ills of this natural female phase
and emerging from it with greatly improved health.

WOMAN'S CHANGE OF LIFE

*Prepared and produced by the Editorial Committee
of Science of Life Books*

Revised and Extended by
Leonard Mervyn B.Sc., Ph.D., F.R.S.C.

SCIENCE OF LIFE BOOKS
11 Munro Street, Port Melbourne, Victoria 3207

Sixth Edition, revised, enlarged
and reset, January 1983

© SCIENCE OF LIFE BOOKS 1983

*Registered at the G.P.O. Sydney
for transmission through the post
as a book*

Inquiries should be made to the publishers:
Lothian Publishing Company Pty. Ltd., 11 Munro Street,
Port Melbourne, 3207

U.K. Distributors:
THORSONS PUBLISHING GROUP
Wellingborough, Northamptonshire, NN8 2RQ

British Library Cataloguing in Publication Data

Woman's change of life.—6th ed.
1. Menopause
I. Science of Life Books. *Editorial Committee*
612'.665   RG186

ISBN 0-909911-98-3

National Library of Australia card number
and ISBN 0 909911 98 3

Printed in Great Britain by
Richard Clay Limited, Bungay, Suffolk.

9 11 13 15 17 19 20 18 16 14 12 10 8

Contents

Foreword

The change of life or menopause, the cessation of the ability to bear children is a normal function occurring during 'middle age' in all women. Some look forward to it, others fear it, but none can avoid it.

The menopause usually occurs over several years between the ages of 40 and 55 years; the actual age is influenced by race, genetic factors, the state of health of the individual and their life-style. It should be looked upon as a great step forward with the same excitement that a teenager has looking forward to adulthood. Unfortunately, many women cling to what they know and are plagued with erroneous fears that the change of life heralds the end of their sex life and their femininity and doubts that their husband will continue to show them love and affection because they can no longer bear children. There is also the fear of physical decline and the onset of old age. No woman wants to age prematurely or, for that matter, grow old at all. There is an old saying that 'a woman is as old as she looks'. Some women look old at 30 while some grandmothers of 70 still possess a radiance and charm to be envied by many of those years younger than themselves.

The secret of coping with middle age and with the menopause is to understand it, to appreciate what is happening in the body and to assist the natural transformation into a new stage of maturity and a new and exciting phase in every woman's life. The more we understand what is happening during the menopause and the more we can assist nature in achieving her ultimate goal, the less stressful this time will be.

During the menopause many women go through severe physical upheaval; there may be hot flushings, weight increase, floodings, anaemia or thyroid trouble, all of which cause a great deal of unpleasantness and concern. Old wives tales do little to help and usually contribute to the anxiety and confusion of many unfortunate sufferers.

The post-menopausal period should be the golden years of womanhood. However, all too often these are marred by complaints such as arthritis, hypertension, diabetes etc., which can begin during the menopause and continue after it is completed if the 'change of life' is not managed properly.

The change of life is not a disease; it is not a condition which requires treatment and yet medicine may be helpful in assisting to relieve some of the uncomfortable symptoms which accompany it. If the menopause is managed successfully these symptoms should never reach a severity which requires medication.

During the menopause menstruation ceases, the glandular system undergoes a major reorganization, the ovarian secretions change and, if this change takes place gradually as nature intended it to, then the fortunate woman passes through the menopause with only minor upsets, a minimum of discomfort and no post-menopausal disorders. However, if any of the glandular secretions change or cease abruptly, then there is a major upheaval and, if the body does not settle down to normality the resultant physical symptoms may be accompanied by psychological problems too.

Every woman should prepare for the menopause. A woman who is well nourished, has a well balanced family relationship, who is able to relax and enjoy life and cope with her life-style is in a much better position to go through the change of life without undue discomfort.

The psychological stress placed on the single woman is no less and sometimes even greater than that experienced by married women. The fear of never being able to find a partner once their ability to bear children ceases is often a very real one, and the added prospect of being left alone in old age suddenly appears as a distinct possibility. Single women approaching the menopause need to be involved with other people.

Their participation in social groups, sporting activities etc. should be encouraged. Sometimes this requires a special effort as it is very easy during the late 30s to settle into a stagnant type of life-style. An unmarried woman, no matter whether she is 20 or 60 should always look forward enthusiastically to what life has to offer her.

Another important factor often neglected by women approaching middle age, is exercise. Exercise is very important in maintaining normal circulation and other physiological functions during the menopause. It is so easy when not feeling well to neglect adequate exercise.

Exercise does not have to be of the extremely strenuous kind; swimming, walking briskly, playing games such as golf, tennis etc. are all good forms of exercise, although when playing competitive sports against another person it is wise to choose a person around the same age as yourself. Many sporting injuries occur as a result of older people playing competitive sports against those who are years younger than themselves. Sports and exercise should be enjoyable. If you are not the athletic type, begin by exercising a few minutes a day and gradually increase the sessions until you are exercising for at least one hour each day. This does not have to be done in one session and can be worked into the normal day's activities. For example a 10 or 15 minute exercise period at night and in the morning, walking briskly to and from work, swimming several times each week and playing some form of active sport at weekends makes it a fairly easy task to average at least one hour's physical activity each day.

The diet is important too. Without adequate nutrition no woman can hope to go through the menopause without problems. One of the problems frequently encountered in middle age is an increase in weight. As soon as signs of weight increase occurs most women become concerned and look for a 'slimming diet', and all too often they are persuaded to follow an unbalanced diet which provides an inadequate level of nutrition.

The information contained in this book is designed to help every woman maintain a high level of nutrition without using a diet which promotes overweight; not only will it help you to adjust your diet but also your life-style so that you will be better able to cope with the change of life and look forward to those 'golden years' at the end of the menopausal rainbow.

1

What is the Menopause?

The menopause, also known as the change of life or the
climacteric, is that period of a woman's life between her
child-bearing years and the time she ceases to
menstruate.

It is true that a great many women have a very distressing experience during the menopause. They suffer
one or two years of very indifferent health. But worse
than the physical ills are the periods of black depression,
and those nameless fears that sit heavily on the mind and
give rise to the feeling that the best in life is over.

Every woman has heard so much of these distressing
symptoms that she approaches the same period as
though she were about to pass through a great crisis that
will not only change her life but change it completely and
for the worse. Let me say at once that this attitude is not
in any way justified by the facts. It is not a great crisis in a
woman's life. It merely marks the end of her child-
bearing capacity, which, after the age of 45 or 50, is

greatly to be desired by every woman. It need not be a period of ill health. With sound nutrition in preparation for it, and in passing through it, a woman's health can be quite satisfactory except for minor readjustments.

It does not mean the end of a woman's sex life, or love life. On the contrary, after about a year of doubtful sex interest, the menopause is usually followed by increased enjoyment because now there is no longer the fear of pregnancy.

The menopause does not mean that a woman's attraction will fade rapidly now that her ovarian rhythm is ended. Finally, it does not mark the beginning of a decline in health to old age, nor is it responsible for any notable increase in the mortality rate among women.

Despite their reservations about the menopause, a recent survey has indicated that many women actually look forward to it. Men and women were asked which age they regarded as the prime of life. Most of the men replied 'about thirty-five' but the women chose 'forty-five plus' when 'they had got the children off their hands'. It seems that most women enjoy life better after the menopause rather than before it.

The side effects of the menopause are not confined to women. In Oxford recently two eminent doctors from the Department of Community Medicine sent question-naires to more than a thousand women and five hundred men in the 30-64 age group, asking about particular symptoms associated with the menopause. They enquired about hot flushes, headaches, skin tingling, sexual problems, backache, mild mental symptoms such as irritability, loss of confidence, difficulty in micturition (passing water) and loss of the ability to fall asleep easily.

What emerged was that both men and women had

these problems fairly frequently. The predominant symptoms amongst menopausal women turned out to be hot flushes, cold sweats, loss of confidence and difficulty in making decisions. Hence, if we regard the men as controls in this study, it is obvious that many of the so-called side effects of the menopause are simply the symptoms of advancing age and will occur at certain times of life whether the female is undergoing the change or not.

The inability to make decisions is perhaps not so surprising. Most women find that they have reached a turning point in their roles as wives and mothers as the age of the menopause approaches. They often face all kinds of difficulties and uncertainties, arising from the fact that loved ones are not quite so dependent on them as they were. The fears are more psychological than physical and are often not helped by unfounded advice from elsewhere.

Without Fear the 'Change' Might Pass Unnoticed

It is the multiplicity of these fears which do most of the mischief at this period. They have been perpetuated by 'old wives' from time immemorial. There are women who get a sort of sadistic pleasure out of telling younger women of the hell that's in store for them during the menopause — the same sort of pleasure that some people get from passing on, and adding to a piece of gossip or scandal.

Also, of course, some writers have themselves painted harrowing pictures of the pains and penalties of the change of life. But the general consensus of medical opinion is that the fears are entirely without foundation, and that with a sound health regimen a woman can pass through this period of adjustment without being either a burden to herself, her family or her friends.

What are the Normal Signs?
What should a woman expect to happen as she approaches the menopause? There is either an increased frequency of menstruation or a larger gap between periods. Hot flushes can occur and sweating can break out even on the slightest physical exertion. Often though, these signs manifest themselves at night when lying in bed and they are usually worse at period times. There is increasing irritability and tiredness and the woman may find a lessening in her vaginal secretions, leading to dryness and subsequent difficulty during intercourse. Of course, there are other symptoms too, but it is highly unlikely that any one woman will experience all of them. This was confirmed in one particular study reported below.

An English Investigation
It is interesting to recall that some years ago a group of women doctors in England, under the auspices of the Medical Women's Federation, examined one thousand women who had recently passed through the change of life, and took records from all of them as to how they had been personally affected by it.

The women who were interrogated represented every class of society — rich and poor, married and single, sick and healthy.

The result of the examination of the thousand women showed that:

160 had no symptoms whatever.
620 experienced flushings.

450 experienced headaches.

400 experienced giddiness.

310 experienced nerves.

240 experienced moods and depression.

210 experienced bad floodings.

340 put on considerable weight.

Not one woman questioned had had all the foregoing symptoms. Most had had only two or three of them, and a great many only had them on a few occasions. The majority said that they had the symptoms in a very mild form. It is important to note that 160 went through the change of life without experiencing any of the above symptoms at all.

The report also stated that only about 100 — one in ten — were so affected by the symptoms that they required relief from their domestic duties or had to give up their employment.

If that was how little the menopause affected women some years ago — before the new science of nutrition was known — there is no reason why any woman today, armed with the new knowledge, should be more than slightly inconvenienced.

It is surprising in view of what can happen during the menopause that so many women can sail through it with no symptoms at all. They may look back some time later and only then realize that menstruation has ceased. The golden rule is this: two years after her last period if she is under 50 or one year after her last period if she is over 50, a woman may safely conclude that she is past the menopause.

Symptoms of the Menopause

The first unmistakable symptoms that a woman is

entering the menopause are irregularity in the monthly periods and reduced menstrual flow. The irregularity is rather disconcerting at first, because the first fear that enters a woman's head is that the non-appearance of the periods at the usual time of the month may mean pregnancy — which is not to be lightly or happily regarded after 40. After a few false alarms it usually dawns upon a woman, even in the absence of medical advice, that she is entering the change of life.

The most normal condition during the change of life is for the menstrual flow to gradually become less and less each month until it finally ceases altogether — a process which should take from two to three years. Some women find the monthly periods end abruptly, with little or no previous warning, and sometimes the periods may occur at longer intervals of five, six, seven or eight weeks. Towards the end of the menopause it is not unusual for the periods to come on at intervals of once or twice a year.

Recent thinking attributes only one specific symptom with the menopause, namely hot flushes. In a paper entitled 'Menopause Myths', Dr C. Wood, reporting in *The Medical Journal of Australia* in 1979, found that when he analyzed twenty symptoms commonly attributed to the menopause, only hot flushes were specifically associated with the condition.

Hot flushes begin shortly after the ovaries cease to function. They are precipitated by emotional upsets, hot drinks and meals, a warm room or bed, and alcohol. The classic description by Dr Glaevecke in 1889 has not been bettered: '. . .the hot flush starts with a kind of aura, with a discomfort in the lower or upper middle part of the abdomen, often with a chill, followed quickly by an intense hot feeling ascending towards the head. The affected skin, mainly the face, becomes red. This is accompanied by anxiety and unease in the heart and stomach areas. After a short interval, a variable amount of sweat breaks out. A feeling of exhaustion ends the attack'.

The cause of hot flushes is not known. Although ovarian extracts and later oestrogens have been regarded as specific treatment, since the beginning of the century, recent research indicates that the levels of the female sex hormones, the oestrogens, in the blood are not directly related to hot flushes. Moreover, it has not been possible to associate any hormonal factor with the appearance of the condition. In a study reported in *The British Journal of Obstetrics and Gynaecology* in 1981, more than 75.1 of women suffering from hot flushes were cured by a placebo (a harmless treatment contributing no drugs but believed by the patient to be therapy).

Menopausal women are commonly over-sensitive to heat, feeling warm when other members of their family do not, dressing more lightly than before the menopause, and becoming uncomfortable or exhausted in hot weather. They may complain of hot waves passing over the whole body and some are plagued by profuse sweating at night, necessitating several changes of night clothes. These observations suggest that malfunction of the temperature-regulating processes of the body plays a part during the menopause, particularly as heat sensitivity arises even in menopausal women who do not have hot flushes.

At What Age Can the 'Change' be Expected?
The age at which the change of life began in the thousand women questioned varied as follows:

Before 40 years	12.5 per cent
From 40 to 45 years	28 per cent
From 46 to 50 years	47 per cent
After 50 years	12.5 per cent

Incidentally, the examination of the thousand women referred to revealed that there were practically no differences between the married and the unmarried, whether childless or not, nor did the age when periods first began seem to have any noticeable influence on the time when the 'change' occurred.

The time varies with different races, climates, and the individual differences in women; one school of medical thought says that an early menopause is due to inadequate secretion of the thyroid gland. But, as the table indicates, a lot of women fall into the 45 to 50 age bracket.

How Long Does the Menopause Last?

Most women ask this question with a great deal of anxiety, but as we have seen, once the unreal fears are set at rest, the health built up to the maximum, and symptoms of the 'change' known and understood, the fact that the menopause takes one or two years is of small moment.

The woman who knows the facts about it and who is prepared for it, physically and mentally, will find little to embarass or disturb her.

Dr Kisch quotes the following figures concerning the duration of the 'change of life' in several hundred cases of which records were kept:

12 per cent of cases	6 months
23 per cent of cases	12 months
37 per cent of cases	18 months

| 19 per cent of cases | 2 years |
| 9 per cent of cases | 3 years |

The average time taken from the first symptoms to the complete cessation of menstruation is about 18 months to two years.

How Some Women Can Cope with the Menopause

Why do some women go through the menopause without any symptoms while others seem to have terrible problems? A lot depends on luck but even more important are the woman's personality and attitude to life. A cheerful, adaptable woman who is busy and satisfied with her husband, her job and her children will find it easier to cope. Other factors contribute to the situation too. These may be financial, inability to manage both a full-time job and run a home, and perhaps difficult children at an age when they came upon adolescent problems. Sometimes there are problems associated with her husband's job, his health or simply his advancing age. All these difficulties which may not be connected with the menopause in a physical sense often crop up at about the same time and, in turn, can lead to a lot of stress and anxiety which will make minor symptoms worse.

There is another aspect which affects women in middle age, a turning point has been reached from which there is no going back. The motherly woman who has longed for a baby and has put off child-bearing because of shortage of money or her husband's negative attitude has now to accept the bleak fact that she will never have a child. At the other end of the scale is the fortunate woman who has fulfilled her expectations sexually and as a mother, or who has an absorbing career, may hardly notice the menopause and actually welcome it as the end of her messy, unpredictable periods and the risk of pregnancy.

When women reach the age of the menopause they have also usually reached the peak of their career and earning powers. They feel the need to consolidate their position rather than break new ground. Such a situation can be hard to accept for someone who feels she has not fulfilled her potential and feels she has missed something out of life.

Some of the appeal of Hormone Replacement Therapy (HRT) is the suggestion that perhaps hormones might preserve a woman's youth and beauty and postpone the trials of advancing age. Later in the book we shall discuss this form of treatment which is usually successful in overcoming the symptoms of the menopause but which still has a question mark relating to its safety.

The Physiology of the Menopause

So that every woman will understand what is happening to her during the menopause, it is important that she has a simple knowledge of the physiology of her ovarian system.

As a girl, every child is equipped with two diminutive internal organs called ovaries, containing about 150,000 microscopic rudimentary egg-cells at the time of birth. Most of these die off during childhood, until by the time puberty arrives the ovaries — which have grown to be the size of an almond — contain about 25,000 such cells of 'ova' (eggs).

Even this, of course, constitutes an enormous over-endowment; for while each ovum is capable, if fertilized by a male sperm cell, of developing into a human being, only a very few are ever so fertilized in the course of a woman's whole child-bearing period, for only some four hundred out of that vast number of ova will leave the ovaries, at the rate of one a month.

The basic difference between the male and female life cell is most interesting. The female child is born with her life supply of egg cells, whereas the spermatozoa or male sperms are created in the male as a continuous process.

Nature is most prolific. It requires only one ovum or egg cell to be fertilized by one male sperm to produce a child, but the woman whose family is usually limited from one to a dozen produces over 400 ova in a lifetime and the male ejaculates millions of sperms at each sexual union, any one of which may fertilize the female ovum.

The fact that the female is endowed with her supply of ova at birth may be responsible for the incidence of sterility amongst women. Ill health or disease — particularly a penetrating venereal disease — is capable of destroying her supply of egg cells before one is fertilized and brought to birth as a human being.

The egg cells lie dormant in the girl for some twelve or fifteen years, and then nature decides that the time has arrived to make a wonderful change. The girl passes from the rather gawky, unshapely, uninteresting phase in her early teens to the strange new world of puberty.

The First Change of Life
When the age of twelve years or so is reached, one of the tiny cells that have lain dormant in the ovary since the birth of the female ripens and travels along the fallopian tube to the womb (uterus). Eventually the process will occur regularly every month but at first the time intervals may be a little longer. However, before that egg

reaches the womb, certain changes have taken place in its lining and these changes are due to the sex hormones that are secreted by every female.

What happens is that the ovary, as well as storing eggs, also produces the female sex hormone called oestrogen which enters the blood from where it is carried to the uterus. Here it has the side effect of thickening the lining of the womb, producing a profusion of new blood vessels in a period of intense activity. A second sex hormone known as progesterone follows closely behind oestrogen and it too acts upon the uterine lining. The net result of the action of these two hormones is to prepare the uterus to receive the fertilized egg. Hence, if the female egg has been fertilized by the male sperm (and this usually happens in the fallopian tube), the fertilized egg travels down to the womb where it becomes embedded in the newly prepared lining, and from that beginning a baby will develop.

If the female egg is not fertilized, it will continue to travel down to the womb, but it does not have the ability to latch on to the lining and it eventually passes out of the vagina. Once this happens, the ovary turns off its supply of the two hormones and the lining of the womb starts to disintegrate. The thickened lining is thus shed and, as it also has a rich vascular system, bleeding occurs at the same time. This is known as menstruation or the menses (the latin name for month) as it happens approximately every four weeks. The common name is the period. The time when menstruation starts in the young girl is known as the menarche. When it stops some thirty or forty years later it is the menopause.

The whole process which starts again immediately after the period is called the menstrual cycle. The two hormones oestrogen and progesterone are in turn controlled by other hormones that are made in the gland known as the pituitary which is situated at the base of the brain. The process goes on through all the child-bearing years and only stops when the woman is pregnant or when the egg cells finally become too old to be fertilized. This results in the second change of life which we have seen is the menopause.

The sex hormones produced by the ovary have a profound effect upon the lining of the womb but they also have other important functions; they change the young twelve-year-old girl into a young woman.

The change in her from the pre-adolescent stage is often breath-taking. The surplus fat falls away, the figure takes shape, the bust develops and, with it, a conscious-ness of sex and all that it implies permeates her life. These changes are induced by the female sex hormones and they are the factors that give a woman those subtle qualities of femininity.

What Happens at the Menopause?

In due time, she reaches the period of her second change of life, the menopause. What happens then? Menstrua-tion gradually ceases, and with it the ovarian secretions diminish. It is the stoppage of certain ovarian secretions which is responsible for most of the physical symptoms of the menopause. If these ovarian secretions diminish gradually the fortunate woman usually passes through the menopause with minor upsets. If these secretions stop abruptly — as they do sometimes — the unfortunate woman has an unhappy year or two.

In such cases it is the medical practice now to prescribe oestrogen. The ovarian secretion largely consists of oestrogen and when the synthetically prepared hormone is given, it has the effect of modifying the symptoms of the menopause. The taking of oestrogen, however, cannot delay the onset of the menopause or put it off altogether.

All the glands of the body are interrelated. They are fed by the blood, and for their efficient functioning the glands need a highly vitaminized diet. As the ovarian secretions diminish, so the other glands take over added activities and thus compensate for lack of ovarian secretion. Summed up, the change of life or menopause is simply the natural termination of a woman's child-bearing period.

The Psychology of the Menopause

The psychological ills of the menopause are probably worse than the physical ills. In the great majority of cases, women at this time find the physical ills quite endurable — that is to say, only a very small percentage of women have to give up their job or go to bed. Some 98 per cent of the thousand women who were questioned by English doctors were able to carry on with their duties right through the menopause without so much as a day in bed.

However, most women agree that it is the psychological — or mental — factors which give them most worry during the change: the days, sometimes weeks, of depression; the feelings of emptiness, inadequacy, hopelessness, self-pity, moodiness and melancholia. Such emotional turns often find women at this time giving way to tears on the slightest provocation, or without any apparent cause at all. In other women, the most common feelings are those of irritability, frustration, tenseness and exasperation. In others, exhaustion is the worst symptom — a feeling of utter incapacity for the daily tasks. Yet others are disturbed and unsettled, a burden to themselves and their families.

In a few women — very few — there is the feeling that their minds are giving way and the year is like a nightmare, although it is likely that this small percentage of women were always a little off balance mentally. Some women suffer from a feeling of unwantedness at this time and are consumed with self-pity. Still others are nervy to the point of 'nervous breakdown'. A few women suffer a mixture of all these varying moods, others only a few. The very fortunate, will experience none at all.

Changes of Life Suffering is Due to Ignorance

Most psychological worries during the menopause are due to the many groundless fears which women harbour in secret dread. Their fears, practically all their mental suffering at this time, are due to their ignorance of the whole phenomenon called the 'Change of Life' since many women enter this phase of their lives without any sound knowledge of what is going to happen to them. Apart from a vague understanding that her monthly periods are going to cease and that her child-bearing days are numbered, she often knows nothing about this process. Nevertheless, the woman fears everything: she fears that her sex life will end; she fears that she will cease to interest her husband; she fears that her health will go into a decline; she fears that her mind may give way; she fears that life after the 'change' will not be worth living.

Now, none of these fears has a vestige of substance. Not one of these things need result as the outcome of her change of life. Every woman can set her mind

completely at rest so far as those five fears are concerned.
Once a woman knows what is happening to her physically, once she knows that her fears are 'old wives' tales',
once she is armed with the knowledge that will prepare
her health for the change of life and build it up for the
useful and interesting years beyond it, then the
menopause loses all its terrors and the adjustment is
made without needless mental and physical suffering.

In fact, that is the three-fold purpose of this book.
Once the ordinary woman knows what she is 'in for'
during the menopause, she can generally bear with
herself and her problems with reasonable equanimity. At
least, she knows what is happening to her, and she
entertains no fearsome fallacies.

Perhaps the worst feeling for a woman is that she
usually goes through this difficult period of
readjustment alone. Obviously, she can rarely take her
children into her confidence. They cannot be expected
to understand these matters. But she should see that her
husband knows the position and understands. Every
husband should read this book, for example, as
understanding will dissipate any strange notions he
might have about the change of life, and will help him to
bear with his wife in her moods. She wants no more than
this understanding and the patience and the sympathy
that should go with it.

Given those three precious things, the period of readjustment can be passed through with the very minimum
of psychological and physical upset.

Sex Life and the Menopause

The sexual relationship between man and woman
naturally becomes more moderate as they grow older.

That is as it should be. During the menopause, the woman goes through a year or two of sexual uncertainty. She may not be by any means her best self, she is often worried by the fear of an undesired pregnancy at this stage — a fear heightened by the irregularity of her periods. Hence, her attitude to sexual intercourse with her husband at this stage is generally one of diffidence. Nevertheless, women vary greatly in their reactions to sexual intercourse during the menopause. To some it becomes uninteresting; to others it may become unpleasant; in yet other cases, sex interest is dormant, while some women have an increased desire. But after the menopause, the average woman develops a new sex vitality, due to the fact the menstruation no longer takes its monthly toll.

There is a popular notion that women are particularly fertile, or prone to conceive, during the change of life. There is no sound basis for this belief. What really happens is that some women, after menstruation has temporarily ceased for two or three months, discard all contraceptive precautions too soon, and conception may then, naturally, take place.

What about Contraception?
The onset of the menopause is often a worry to many women because, although it signals the end of their child-bearing years, there is still the nagging thought that, in the interim period before absolute cessation of her egg production, there must always be the possibility than an egg is secreted and fertilization may ensue. Even during the period of less frequent ovulation the chance is always there. This is a very important aspect of middle-age.

At this stage, efficient birth control is more important than ever. Most women have the ability to conceive until well beyond 40 years of age but, for social and medical reasons, having a baby at this stage in life is not a very good idea. What then should she do to prevent this happening? The contraceptive pill which a woman may have used during her early years should not be taken by those over 40. If a woman smokes, this age can be reduced to 35. The reason is that the contraceptive pill increases the risk of a stroke or heart disease in women over the age of 35 or so. The older the woman is, the greater her risk in using this form of contraception.

The coil or intrauterine device (IUD) is a very efficient and useful method for many women that can be used right into the menopause. Some women may find that the coil induces heavy bleeding or it may cause an excessive amount of infection, and in either case the method is not recommended. In the absence of these two complications, however, the coil represents a safe method of contraception.

The cap and the sheath have no side effects and, when used correctly, their safety level approaches that of the pill and coil. When used with an efficient spermicidal jelly, the cap has a 98 per cent success rate. The sheath is only slightly lower at 97 per cent.

The ultimate technique must be sterilization of one or other of the partners. Once they have completed their families it is now relatively easy for either the man or the woman to be sterilized by a simple operation. This is often a wise decision, but adequate discussion and counselling is needed even in a good stable marriage. There is no reason why modern techniques cannot effectively sterilize a woman without upsetting her hormone balance so that there is no premature menopause.

The Artificial Menopause

So far, I have discussed the natural menopause. We use the term 'artificial menopause' for those cases in which the ovaries have had to be removed because of some diseased condition, often long before the woman has reached middle life.

It is as well that there should be a clear idea in the minds of most women of what constitutes artificial menopause. There are cases in which women, following illness, accident or shock, may cease to menstruate, some for a time and some permanently. In some cases, menstruation will return and the woman will suffer no more than the very minor symptoms of the menopause.

When menstruation ceases permanently — and prematurely — however, all the symptoms of the menopause will be experienced and, due to the abrupt stoppage of menstruation, the symptoms, regardless of the age of the woman concerned, will generally be more difficult than when the menopause has come normally and gradually. In cases such as these, it is the practice nowadays for doctors to prescribe oestrogen treatment to modify the symptoms.

Where the uterus is removed and the ovaries are left unmolested, the woman ceases to menstruate but the symptoms of the menopause are not likely to develop until the change of life would otherwise begin. This, of course, is due to the important fact that the ovaries are still present.

The Causes of Artificial Menopause

An artificial menopause is often due to the ovaries ceasing to function long before the normal change of life often because they have been infected by some serious infectious disease, such as typhoid, cholera, pneumonia, tuberculosis, pernicious anaemia, leukaemia (deficiency of red blood corpuscles), diabetes or venereal disease.

An artificial menopause may also be due to X-ray treatment destroying the germinal layer of the ovaries, or it may be due to shock or to a too rapid series of confinements. In certain cases, where malignant fibroid growth is suspected, both ovaries and all ovarian tissue are removed by surgical operation.

In younger women the ovaries are removed or destroyed when they are diseased. Sometimes patients with cancer of the breast have the ovaries destroyed by X-ray to lower the level of oestrogen in the blood.

An artificial menopause can be unpleasant as the sudden change in hormone levels is often followed by many hot flushes, sweats and depression. Treatment is the same for these conditions as for the natural menopause, and this is discussed later.

However, the operation known as hysterectomy — removal of the womb or uterus — does not produce such drastic changes. The ovaries are still intact and so they continue to produce egg cells each month. Hormones are still secreted by the ovaries so the usual monthly cycle of hormone changes occurs. This commonly causes water retention, swelling of the breasts and pre-menstrual tension before the time the normal period would be, but of course there is no bleeding. During the week in which the period would have started the woman tends to pass more urine to get rid of the excess fluid that would normally be lost in menstruation.

2

The Problems of the Menopause

Now let us deal, in more detail, with the physical symptoms of the menopause period.

First, 'hot flushes'. This is the most common symptom of the change of life. They sometimes occur before the periods become irregular, or they may be noticed months after the periods have ceased. Usually, however, 'hot flushes' occur during the year or two in which the monthly flow is coming to an end.

One woman in three, goes through the menopause without experiencing hot flushing at all. Others say that the discomfort is very slight. The length of time over which the individual may suffer hot flushes varies between weeks and years. In exceptional cases, they may have intermittent flushing for ten years or more. The most common period is, however, nearer two years.

There is no certain answer to the question of what causes hot flushing. Some doctors hold that it is due to the lowered quantities of oestrogen failing to counteract certain stimuli coming from the pituitary gland, and it is felt that it is related to loss or insufficiency of the internal secretions of the ovaries.

What can be done to minimize flushing? Some doctors give ovarian extract, and it has been suggested that where there is insufficient ovarian activity, the symptom can usually be effectively treated by giving ovarian hormone (oestrogen).

It is often believed that the quicker a woman works through the hot flush period, the sooner she stops having them. Oestrogen treatment merely postpones their ending. This is probably true, as giving oestrogen tablets usually cures the flushing temporarily, but it does return, often quite severely, after the treatment has ended. For this reason, it is usual to reduce the hormone treatment gradually and wait until cool weather before stopping it altogether.

Flushing is nearly always worse in hot weather, and when conditions of stress and anxiety are prevalent. Alcohol and hot beverages also contribute to the severity of the condition. Often, a cool shower or bath or even a simple sponge-down before bedtime is beneficial. Light bed linen and night-dresses made of cotton are preferable to the heavy varieties, particularly when these are made from synthetic fabrics.

We shall see later how oestrogen therapy may not be necessary for treating hot flushes during the menopause, since comparable beneficial results have been obtained with vitamin E. According to the Shute Institute of Canada who are the leading researchers in the field of vitamin E, the vitamin exerts its action in females by normalizing the blood levels of oestrogens. At the same time, vitamin E improves the heat-regulating capacity of the body which is believed to be upset during the menopause. Any imbalance in this control will result in hot flushes and sweating that are symptoms of this condition.

Head Noises and Headaches

About half the women who go through the menopause complain of headaches, head noises and/or giddiness. Sometimes the head noises consist of a constant 'ringing in the ears' known as tinnitus. This condition is not confined to the menopause, but is suffered by many members of the population, both male and female. However, it is often a feature of the menopause, appearing only during the period of the actual change.

Similarly, the general incidence of headache is probably not much greater than is usually suffered by women, but head noises are different. They can be a definite menopausal symptom due to the upset in the functioning of the glands. As well as tinnitus, the head noises may take the form of a confused rushing sound which may be continuous.

Unfortunately, medical science has no answer to head noises and the usual treatment is mild tranquillizers which help only in occasional cases. Similarly, headaches are usually treated with analgesics such as aspirin and paracetamol which may remove the pain but do nothing to alleviate the cause. We must therefore look to dietary or natural treatments of both head noises and headaches and, fortunately, these have a greater chance of success than conventional drug therapy.

A high potency vitamin B-complex taken regularly will often alleviate both head noises and headaches. Doses vary considerably and where one individual may require only 10mg quantities of vitamins B^1, B^2 and B^6 with 50mg quantities of calcium pantathenate (B^5) and nicotinamide (B^3), others may require up to ten times these potencies to relieve their symptoms. Vitamin B^{12} taken in addition can also help but there is little virtue in taking more than 25mcg daily as absorption of the vitamin into the body is very limited. Intramuscular injection of B^{12} will give higher body levels but this is the province of the practitioner. Injections of this vitamin alone have sometimes helped, but the best treatment is to take the whole of the vitamin B complex orally. There are ample preparations available to the sufferer with potencies varying as described above. The complex should be taken either as divided doses (i.e. one with each meal) or as a prolonged-release preparation to ensure that blood levels of the vitamins are maintained at a high concentration over the day.

Varicose Veins

During the climacteric the blood vessels often become the seat of what are technically known as engorgements, but what we may render in more familiar terms as 'impeded circulation', often resulting in varicose veins. This may occur in all parts of the body, but is particularly frequent in the arms and legs, hands and feet, fingers and toes, especially in the morning, or in low temperatures.

Varicose veins occur most often in the legs. The leg veins, the largest in the body, carry blood back to the heart for recirculation through the lungs. The blood in the leg veins moves upwards against the force of gravity, hence the blood pressure is slight. Leg veins are provided with valves, each consisting of two pockets or flaps to keep the blood flowing upwards. These valves, when in health, operate to prevent blood moving downwards towards the feet.

When a leg becomes weakened for any of the reasons mentioned below, the valves in the vein fail to meet across it, allowing space for blood to move in either direction. This can result in a vein becoming inflamed, swollen, knotted and tortuous. It is then known as a varicose vein.

(a) During the change of life the muscles tend to become lax and flabby. The walls of the veins, like other tissues, tend to lose their elasticity and start to dilate, allowing stagnant blood to accumulate. If not corrected, varicose veins and later varicose ulcers may develop.

(b) During pregnancy, some women suffer painful varicosities. The inflamed veins are the result of increased weight, pelvic congestion and pressure. These inflamed veins often become normal after delivery.

(c) Constipation has also been cited as a primary cause of varicose veins. The inevitable delay in the passage of colonic contents results in extra 'weight', which in turn arrests the flow of blood in even the largest veins.

Food and Varicose Veins

According to Dr Denis Burkitt, a surgeon of international renown, the diet is one of the main factors in determining the development of varicose veins. After studying both primitive and 'civilized' communities throughout the world, Dr Burkitt has concluded that the amount of dietary fibre in the diet is all-important.

Dietary fibre consists of the portion of food that is not digested by normal body processes, and it is made up of bran from cereals plus cellulose from vegetables and fruits. The function of dietary fibre is to absorb water which makes it swell and hence becomes a natural bulking agent. By supplying this indigestible bulk, dietary fibre allows the muscles of the intestines a solid substance on which to contract and so makes the passage of the food easier as it moves down the digestive tract.

In the absence of bulk in the diet, the intestinal muscles have nothing solid to grip and they become lax and flaccid. Instead of moving smoothly down the intestine, the food lags behind and its rate of passage slows down. Lack of dietary fibre also means that it loses water by reabsorption in the large intestine so that the stools, when they become ready for excretion, are small and hard instead of smooth and moist. Defaecation then becomes difficult and straining of the muscles has a number of consequences.

The increased abdominal pressure caused by this straining has been singled out as a major cause of haemorrhoids (piles) and varicose veins. Constipation produced by a lack of dietary fibre can also be a cause of diverticulitis. Hence, constipation as a disease in its own right and also as a primary cause of varicose veins, piles and diverticulitis is seen only in those communities that subsist on diets where dietary fibre has been removed by the processing and refining of foods. These diseases are practically unknown where the diet is mainly unrefined and consists of balanced ingredients from a variety of foods. It is also not without significance that these diseases often appear at the time of onset of the menopause because it is at this period of life that the consequence of low-fibre diets over the previous 40 years or so are beginning to have their effects.

It is easier to prevent these diseases than to cure them and prevention is a relatively easy matter. Just ensure a daily intake of wholemeal bread, bran (alone or in the form of cereals), muesli (the nuts and fruits in this are rich in dietary fibre, in addition to that in the wholegrain cereals), leaf and root vegetables, fruits and legumes (peas and beans of all kinds). A diet based on these basic foods will supply sufficient fibre to prevent constipation-related diseases.

Varicose Ulcers
Varicose ulcers develop from neglected varicose veins. If the skin in the lower part of the leg in which varicose veins are present is injured by a cut or bruise, the skin often fails to heal because the blood supply to the area is scanty. In such cases, dermatitis may follow. Varicose veins often cause itching and should the skin be scratched, a moisture may exude, leading to dermatitis. This frequently becomes septic and healing proves difficult. Eczema of the leg may follow, causing ulceration and producing chronic varicose ulcers.

Natural Treatment of Varicose Veins and Ulcers
Vitamin E: An adequate intake of vitamin E throughout the period of life leading up to the menopause will result in a decreased risk of developing varicose veins and ulcers, according to Dr W. Shute in his book *Vitamin E for Ailing and Healthy Hearts*. This is because the vitamin improves the blood circulation by dilating the capillaries. At the same time it strengthens the walls of the blood vessels and the surrounding muscles, thus pre-

venting them from becoming lax and flabby, preconditions in the development of varicose veins. The flow of blood is also improved by vitamin E because of its ability to dissolve blood clots and prevent their formation.

Successful treatment of both varicose veins and varicose ulcers can often be achieved by a daily dose of 150 IU or 300 IU of the natural vitamin which is increased by increments of 100 IU every six weeks if no improvement is noted. Most people respond to a daily intake of 300 or 600 IU, but occasionally the dose must be increased to 800 IU per day before relief is obtained. Once the individual starts responding to vitamin E, the dose at which benefit is obtained may be maintained quite safely. Often, once the condition has cleared, a maintenance intake of 200 or 250 IU of vitamin E will prevent recurrence of the problem. Even in the absence of varicose veins and ulcers, a daily intake of 200 IU or so may well prevent their development. At the same time, varicose ulcers may also be treated with a vitamin E cream or ointment since these will complement the oral therapy.

Vitamin C and the Capillaries

This vitamin strengthens the walls of blood vessels and the connective tissue, known as collagen, in which the cells are embedded. It has a particular function in maintaining healthy capillaries.

When the walls of the capillaries (tiny, hair-like blood vessels that ramify into almost every part of the body) break down through weakness, blood escapes into the tissues, the bone marrow, joints, etc., leading to rheumatic and other ailments.

The capillaries carry food and oxygen to the cells as

well as removing waste products from them. But when supplies of nutrients fail to reach cells, due to broken capillaries, those cells die in a matter of seconds. Dead cells have no protection against bacteria viruses. Instead, the dead cells actually foster the growth of these harmful invaders of the bloodstream, and in this way, dead cells can aid bacterial infection.

Broken capillaries also form a system of transport, enabling bacteria to reach other parts of the body. Bacteria may thus reach the joints, to cause arthritis; the kidneys, to result in kidney ailments; or the heart, to give rise to rheumatic heart disease.

Vitamin C Losses

Vitamin C aids the body in utilizing proteins and fats in the cells. This vitamin is the most vulnerable of any of the vitamin family. It is lost when vegetables are soaked in water and cooked. It is destroyed by DDT used in insecticides and pest sprays; by many of the drugs in common use; by smoking; by smog and smoke; by inhaling petrol fumes and the fumes of cleaning solvents. It is also lost to the body by the action of the components of the contraceptive pill. Prolonged use of this form of contraception can cause losses of vitamin C that can lead to later problems during the menopause. Vitamin C is not stored in the body and must be taken daily to meet the body's demands. Vitamin C also has a unique action in reducing blood cholesterol levels to normal values. It does this by increasing the rate at which cholesterol in the blood is degraded and disposed of. Usually, a daily intake of 500mg of vitamin C should be ensured before and during the menopause, since this potency has been found to be the most efficacious in many clinical studies.

Rutin

This is one of the bioflavonoids and these make up a group of natural substances known as vitamin P. Rutin is helpful in all disorders of the blood circulation. It controls capillary resistance and reduces capillary fragility. Weakened capillaries develop broken walls and allow blood to seep into the surrounding tissues. The condition leads to easy bruising and an excessive tendency to bleed under the skin. Rutin prevents these abnormalities by strengthening the capillary wall.

Rutin has also been found to be of use in the more chronic and serious conditions of hardening of the arteries (arteriosclerosis) and thrombophlebitis (blood clots in the veins), both of which are features of the menopause.

One significant fact is that, in natural foods, bioflavonoids always accompany vitamin C. Hence, it is not surprising perhaps that both substances work together in a synergistic manner, (i.e. the benefits of their contribution are greater than the sum of their individual contributions). Buckwheat is a particularly rich source of rutin, but it is also available in tablet form. One 50mg tablet taken with each meal will complement the 500mg of vitamin C needed to treat varicose veins and ulcers and indeed prevent them.

Nervous Problems

It is quite natural and normal for women at this time to suffer in varying degrees from 'nerves'. The surprising fact is that only about one-third of the women questioned experienced this symptom. For those that do, however, the diet and general design for living, as recommended in this book, usually works like a charm, as most women approach the menopause age suffering from a vitamin- and calcium-starved nervous system.

The deficiency in the B group of vitamins — there are about a dozen vitamins in the B group — is probably the worst factor in the diet of the average man and woman. The richest source of the B vitamins is in the germ of wheat — or rice — but this vital element is removed in the refining of flour and the polishing of rice. The result of this criminal folly concerning the health of the people of all nations is that we are becoming a race of neurotics and neurasthenics; and during the menopause, when a woman is beset by a plague of fears, it is no wonder that her starved nerves go to pieces.

One answer to nervous disorders is 3 dessertspoonsful of wheatgerm with grated apple or raisins and milk for breakfast, and one B¹ (10mg) and one B-complex tablet before each meal.

One other factor essential for sound nerves is calcium. The woman who doesn't average 1 pint (½ litre) of milk and 3 oz (75g) of cheese daily should take two calcium tablets before each meal. (It is not advisable to take sedatives, bromides, 'tranquillizer' drugs, or aspirin for 'nerves' during the menopause.)

It is also true that mental illness is commoner in the elderly than in the young. The sudden changes in hormone levels associated with the menopause may be followed by an attack of depression. However, it must be remembered that real mental illness is no more common during the menopause than at any other time. There is sometimes a small increase in minor nervous complaints, such as slight depression, giddiness or sleeplessness in women during the two years before the periods stop. If these are left untreated there is a tendency for those who already have a history of mental disease to have a nervous breakdown at the time. In a previously healthy person, there is no evidence that a nervous breakdown is associated with the menopause.

A high intake of the whole of the vitamin B-complex often helps to alleviate many of the nervous symptoms associated with the menopause. Of particular benefit, however, is vitamin B^6 which we shall see later has specific functions in maintaining a healthy nervous system. The components of the contraceptive pill are known to have an adverse effect upon the vitamin B^6 status of a woman using it and the deficiency induced can, as with vitamin C, eventually lead to problems in the menopause.

Rheumatism

About one woman in four experiences perhaps her first twinges of rheumatism at the time of the menopause. The rheumatism might be in the muscles or in the joints — the latter being an arthritic condition, and more serious. Rheumatism, in any of its forms, is often the result of the accumulation of acidity or acid end-products in the bloodstream.

The diet of the average person is notorious for its excess of acid-forming foods, such as porridge meals, bread, potatoes, cakes, jam, sugar, biscuits, sweets, and the piquant concoctions of the delicatessen. The diet of the average person tends to be deficient in the vital alkaline foods such as fruit, salad vegetables, fruit juices and dried fruits. It is the excess of the former and the deficiency of the latter which throws the blood out of chemical balance and gives rise to the development of rheumatic symptoms. The tendency to rheumatism in a great many women is present after the age of 45, but during the menopause the tendency is often increased.

A simple and effective answer to rheumatism is the diet recommended in this book, plus one vitamin C tablet (250mg), one B^1 tablet (10mg), one vitamin E tablet (50mg) and one B-complex tablet before each meal (all taken together), and two vitamin A and D capsules taken three times daily after meals. If this diet is adhered to during and after the menopause, rheumatism should not present such a serious problem.

Recent studies reported in *The Practitioner* have confirmed that a high-potency vitamin B intake can help relieve rheumatic symptoms. One particular B vitamin, pantothenic acid, appears to be particularly beneficial. When taken in doses of between 500mg and 2000mg per day, pantothenic acid (in the form of calcium pantothenate) reduced both muscle stiffness and the severity of pain associated with the condition.

Why pantothenic acid should have this beneficial effect is not known with certainty, but one clue may reside in its function in controlling the synthesis of the anti-stress hormones of the body. The production of sex hormones is also dependent on adequate levels of pantothenic acid in the body. Lack of the vitamin results in a lowered rate of synthesis of all these hormones with subsequent development of inflammatory and degenerative diseases associated with the menopause. It is likely that an adequate intake of pantothenic acid during the years leading up to the menopause will ensure against many of the consequences of that condition.

Constipation

Constipation is a universal complaint — 'the father of

diseases'. It is aggravated during the menopause. Constipation, in turn, aggravates the ills of the menopause. Every woman during this period is well advised to make a consistent attempt to rid herself of this menace to her health, without recourse to pills or purgatives. These have caused more troubles than probably any other one factor.

We have seen that constipation is also a cause of other ills and the only sure and satisfactory answer to it is found in the diet. In addition to the types of high-fibre food mentioned previously, the following suggestions are also relevant in preventing constipation and its consequences:

1. Breakfast of wheatgerm, milk, grated apple or stewed fruit (apricots or prunes especially). Wheatgerm is an excellent food and a wonderful aid to bowel regularity.
2. Two apples and cheese for lunch, or a leafy salad.
3. Molasses before retiring.
4. Two B^1 (10mg) and one B-complex tablet before each meal.
5. Cut out all stodgy, constipating foods.

Any woman who includes these suggestions in her diet should never experience constipation again.

Irregular Bleeding

Any irregular bleeding or spotting between periods is a symptom that must be reported to your doctor. Sometimes it occurs after sex and occasionally bleeding appears after the menopause. Whenever it happens outside normal menstruation, the problem of bleeding is one that requires medical advice. A good diet and supplementation with vitamins and minerals can prevent some of the consequences of irregular bleeding, but the cause of the condition must first be diagnosed by a doctor.

Heavy periods which leak through several pads or cause 'floodings' should also be reported, as they may cause anaemia through abnormal loss of iron. Other causes of heavy bleeding are fibroids in the womb or some other disease. Whatever the cause, treatment usually consists of medical drugs or a minor operation called a D and C (i.e. dilation and curettage), which simply means surgical removal of the lining of the womb. More drastic means such as hysterectomy (removal of the womb) may be found to be necessary.

Diet supplementation can be beneficial in reducing the consequences of 'flooding'. The following should be taken three times daily just before or during meals: two vitamin B-complex tablets, one vitamin C (250mg) tablet and one kelp tablet (all together), and after meals two vitamin A and D capsules. Calcium is best obtained from such foods as milk, cheese and lettuce, supplemented by 6 calcium tablets daily. Iron is obtained by substituting wheatgerm for breakfast cereal and adding molasses, eggs, raisins, grapes and apricots (fresh or dried) to the diet. Iron-rich foods include liver, wheatgerm, wholemeal flour, oatmeal, unpolished rice, parsley, prunes, carrots, raw celery, raw onions, apples, bananas, cherries, dates, grapes, orange and lemon juice, peaches, pears, plums, pumpkins, mushrooms, raisins, honey, molasses, salmon (canned), sardines (canned), raw cabbage, lettuce, soya beans, cooked potatoes, spinach, pineapple and tomato. These are all excellent sources of organic iron and are more effective in combating simple anaemia than many iron pills or tonics.

Any excess of iron is stored in the liver, bone marrow,

and spleen. A small proportion of copper, stated to be
about 2mg daily, seems to be necessary to enable iron to
form haemoglobin. However, many foods which contain
iron also contain copper, namely molasses, liver,
apricots, egg yolk, wheatgerm, nuts, spinach, carrots,
leafy vegetables, mushrooms, etc.

Digestive Upsets
Digestive upsets are due to the disturbed glandular
condition. The average woman is 'off-colour', irritable,
easily upset, depressed, and genuinely worried about her
future, and it is not difficult to see that digestive upsets
would follow naturally from a succession of such moods
and stresses.

   However, digestive upsets at this time can be avoided
in most cases, provided fears have been set at rest and
diet is sound, simple, and not deficient in any vitamin or
mineral. Vitamin B^1 tablets are particularly valuable for
good digestion.

   Other measures that may help relieve digestive upsets
during the menopause include digestive enzymes in
tablet form. When taken with a meal they complement
the action of the natural juices. Improving the natural
bacteria of the intestine can also help and this is simply
done by taking freeze-dried bacteria in capsules or
powder form. *Lactobacillus Acidophilus* and *Lactobacillus
bulgaricus* may be taken in this way, and they supplement
the existing bacteria that are normal inhabitants of the
intestines.

Vaginal Problems
Many women find that the first thing they notice as the
menopause approaches is a change in their vaginal se-

cretions. These usually come from the vaginal passage and from the body and the neck of the womb. In most cases, these secretions lessen at the menopause. This, in turn, causes vaginal tightness and soreness although a slight thinning of the skin lining the vagina also contributes to these problems. The simplest treatment is a lubricant jelly used before intercourse. A vitamin E cream is even more effective, particularly when it is combined with high oral doses of vitamin E. A daily supplement of between 400 IU and 600 IU is usually sufficient.

A far more distressing problem is itching and irritation of the vulval region during the menopause. This is a nuisance which may be due to several causes such as thrush, infection, threadworms, allergy to contraceptives, reaction to soap and vaginal sprays and thickening of the vulval skin. Many women destroy and inflame the lining of the vagina with antiseptic or deodorants.

The simplest treatment is to take twice daily baths, bidets or showers, using nothing but warm water. A night sedative is also useful to induce sleep so that you are unable to rub and scratch the affected area. An excellent sedative for restful sleep is dolomite which may be taken in tablet form. This mineral contains magnesium, lack of which causes restlessness, muscle tremor, irritability and sometimes excitability. Alternatively, magnesium alone may be taken just before bed, preferably in the form of an amino acid chelate to guarantee efficient absorption. There are also many excellent herbal remedies to induce sleep. Sometimes the irritation may be due to a mild infection, but treatment for this is best left to your practitioner. Your husband may also have to be treated at the same time to prevent cross-infection during intercourse.

3

Consequences of the Menopause

In the previous chapter, I dealt with some of the more obvious problems a woman going through the menopause might encounter. There are, however, many consequences of the menopause of which she may not yet be aware, although these may be lessened or even avoided by a change in lifestyle, particularly with regard to her diet. The ease with which a woman goes through the menopause may also be related to her mode of life during the years leading up to it. Hence, in order to control any potential consequences of the menopause, we should consider how her lifestyle and dietary habits can determine her ability to cope with her conditon. Let us now examine the first change of life, that of puberty.

Problems of Adolescence

Adolescent girls often suffer from simple anaemia and acne. These two complaints are, to a great degree, associated with the glandular changes which take place during

the transformation from adolescence to adulthood.
These conditions present considerable problems to the
young lady who is now becoming conscious of her
appearance and attractiveness to the opposite sex.

The distress caused by acne and anaemia can, in most
cases, be prevented or greatly helped by an understanding of how these conditions are brought about and the
nutritional changes required to correct them.

Acne
Acne is a blood condition generally associated with adolescence and is thought to be due to the development of
the sebaceous glands at puberty. It occurs in individuals
between 15 to 25 years and is seen in both sexes. Acne
commonly involves the face, back and chest, and takes
the form of blackheads, pimples, pustules, inflammatory
nodules and scarring.

Acne arises from an infection of the cells of the lower
layer of the skin and can cause embarrassment and
mental suffering to sensitive persons. The stresses of
growth, inadequate diet, school pressures and emotional
problems also aggravate the ailment.

Recent scientific research indicates that acne responds
favourably to a carefully planned diet which includes
vitamins and minerals that are frequently deficient in
modern 'convenience' foods. It is recommended that
acne sufferers take the following before meals, three
times a day (all together):
   2 comfrey tablets
   1 lecithin capsule (250mg)
   2 desiccated liver tablets
   1 zinc tablet containing 5mg zinc

Note: Many acne sufferers have, on clinical trial, been found to respond to oral zinc supplementation in addition to the dietary recommendations mentioned below. To avoid irritation of the skin only the mildest herbal soap should be used.

Dietary Information. Certain foods and drinks aggravate acne, namely sweets, chocolates, pastries; greasy and fried foods; spicy foods, seasonings and condiments; all soft drinks and alcoholic beverages. Sausage meats, white flour products, polished rice and such third-rate foods should be eliminated from the diet. Fatty foods to be avoided are milk, cream, ice cream, butter, peanut butter, margarine, potato chips, pork, ham, bacon, creamed soups, gravy and canned fish.

The diet should consist primarily of lean meat, fresh fruits and salad vegetables. Starchy foods should be cut down. Wheatgerm (which is a protein) should be served for breakfast with raisins, honey and milk, or alternatively egg-yolk.

Ointments are better left alone as they rarely giving lasting results, and squeezing, pinching and picking the eruptions should be avoided as the surrounding tissue is thereby injured and healing delayed. The general health should receive attention and conditions such as constipation or anaemia should be rectified.

Simple Anaemia

The anaemic girl is pale and bloodless: she is without appetite and energy because her impoverished bloodstream is not supplying the vital organs with a proper amount of nutritional material. Her whole organism, both physical and mental is affected. She is listless, weary, breathless at the least exertion, and feels incapable.

It is the blood that transports assimilated food and oxygen to all parts of the system where it is oxidized (burned) to produce energy, rebuild tissues, renew bone and tooth structure, and meet other bodily needs.

The body can only make use of this food material if oxygen is present, in the same way that fire cannot burn without oxygen. Oxygen is obtained from the lungs when the red pigment of the blood called haemoglobin unites with oxygen. If, for any reason, the amount of haemoglobin in the blood is low, the blood cannot serve as a good oxygen-carrier and the body is improperly nourished.

A vitally important constituent of haemoglobin is iron. If food iron, that is organic iron, is missing from the diet for any length of time, the amount of blood pigment (haemoglobin) is lowered. This condition is known as nutritional anaemia and is characterized by pallor, listlessness and poor appetite. There may also be dizziness, headaches and poor memory. Thus simple anaemia is not a disease, it is a deficiency condition — a state of bloodlessness due to improper nutrition.

The main cause of simple anaemia in the adolescent girl, and indeed in older women of child-bearing age, is the loss of iron in the blood that accompanies every period. Iron is constantly being lost at the rate of between 0.5 and 1.0mg per day, but during menstruation a further 13.5mg is excreted in the menstrual flow. This means that an extra 0.45mg of iron must be absorbed every day of the month to merely account for this loss. Iron is difficult to absorb at the best of times, but this extra amount must also be found and this is beyond the capability of many women. Hence, they are in an almost permanent state of iron-deficiency anaemia.

Iron tonics are often prescribed, but these invariably contain iron in the inorganic form which is not well absorbed and, for this reason, they often have side effects upon the gastro-intestinal system of cither of the two extremes — constipation or diarrhoea. If you need an iron supplement take it in the organic form, which is how it occurs in food, by ensuring your tablet is an amino-chelated iron. This is more efficiently absorbed because of its organic nature, and for the same reason it does not cause side effects.

Fortunately, most iron supplements are in the ferrous form which is how the mineral is absorbed. Avoid those with iron in the ferric form as this is destructive to vitamin E. Remember, too, that iron from non-meat sources needs vitamin C for efficient absorption and the vitamin must be taken with the meal to ensure this. A good and carefully selected diet, however, should provide all the iron a woman needs but sometimes she may feel the need for extra iron with traces of copper and certain vitamins which are mentioned below.

Simple anaemia requires that the diet includes iron-rich foods such as wheatgerm, liver, yeast, raisins, apricots, molasses, parsley, egg yolk, soybeans, dried fruit, pumpkin and prunes. The body is well adapted to assimilate the organic iron in foodstuffs, and iron in this form does not have any adverse effect upon the vitamins in the body.

Many simple anaemias may be caused by a lack of protein foods so it is important to eat some protein food *at every meal*. The first-class proteins are meat, fish, cheese, eggs, poultry, milk, wheatgerm, brewer's yeast, nuts, soybeans and powdered milk. An egg flip is a palatable and easily assimilated form of protein.

The more serious types of anaemia are called the macrocytic and pernicious anaemias. These require treatment by a physician.

Vitamin dosage for simple anaemia: 1 vitamin B_1 tablet (10mg); B-complex tablet; 2 B_{12} tablets; 1 vitamin C tablet (250mg); 1 kelp tablet; 1 folic acid tablet and 2 desiccated liver tablets, three times daily before meals. Iron (15mg per day) in the organic, amino acid-chelated form, and copper (1mg per day), also in the organic form, may be taken with these vitamins.

Since all anaemias are not necessarily of the iron-deficient type, this should be diagnosed by a physician before self-treatment is attempted. Other types of anaemia require expert advice and are not suitable for self-treatment.

What Iron Means to Health

Iron and oxygen possess a strong attraction for each other. This is why exposed ironwork will soon rust away, unless an artificial skin of paint is placed over it to protect it from the corrosive effect of the oxygen in the atmosphere. Rusting is actually a slow burning process.

Nature has utilized this powerful affinity between iron and oxygen to ensure that oxygen is carried to every part of the body. The function of oxygen is to 'burn up' the nutrients we consume, thereby converting them into energy and bodily heat, and enabling the body to use them for its other purposes.

The red cells in the blood contain an iron-carrying protein called haemoglobin. When air is breathed into the lungs, the oxygen in the air combines with the haemoglobin in the red cells and the result of this affinity is known as oxyhaemoglobin, which is carried through the entire intricate network of blood vessels.

The oxygen-enriched blood is then distributed through the tissue fluids and cells, and some of the oxygen is released to enable the cells to maintain their chemical activities, essential to life. After the release of oxygen, the now deoxygenated blood is returned by the veins to the heart and pumped back to the lungs, where it is again exposed to the revivifying influence of oxygen. This process continues unceasingly while life exists.

Iron Requirements

The daily requirement of iron for an adult, according to A. Davis, should not fall below 15mg.

At least 70 per cent of all iron in the body is contained in the blood, where it exists as haemoglobin. Iron also forms part of the nucleus of each of the trillions of body cells.

The amount of iron in the body is only about one part in every 25,000 of the body's weight, according to A.F. Pattee in *Dietetics*. This authority also states that in a person weighing 10 stone 10 lb, the amount of iron would be approximately a tenth of an ounce, but this small quantity is indispensable to bodily well-being. A lack of iron in the diet causes the skin to take on a pale or yellowish tint, and centuries ago this condition was called chlorosis.

Iron was first discovered in the blood by Mcnghini about 200 years ago, and simple or nutritional anaemia was treated by the physicians of ancient civilizations with water containing iron. There is an old medical treatise which refers to anaemia as 'the disease of the pale ears'.

A female who is constantly iron-deficient during her

menstruating years will carry the deficiency through to the menopause. Assuming she does not suffer from 'floodings' during this period, it might be thought that the reduced menstrual flow associated with the menopause and the ultimate cessation of periods will allow her to retain more iron. This is not always the case, and in fact there is a particular type of iron-deficient anaemia that is associated solely with the menopause.

This type of anaemia is difficult to treat since it is essentially a deficiency due to poor absorption and assimilation of the iron in the diet. It has been established, however, that if a women enters the menopause in a healthy state with her full complement of iron reserves, built up by a sensible diet in her younger years, she is less likely to encounter problems of anaemia in later life.

Stay Well with Protein

The word protein is derived from the Greek *proteios*, meaning primary, and there is no class of foodstuffs of greater importance to bodily health.

Protein is indispensable to life because the human body is largely composed of protein, i.e. the individual cells making up the skin, nails, hair muscles, brain and internal organs, base of the bones, etc. These cells are continually wearing out and breaking down, and unless they are replaced the flesh falls away, the skin wrinkles, and the process of ageing is accelerated.

Protein is vitally important to the body's intelligence system, which appears to be located in the cells, enabling each individual cell to select the precise type of amino acid it needs for its purpose; for use by skin, nail, hair, blood, or for hormones, muscular tissue, etc.

The various types of cells have different functions to

perform, hence their structural composition differs widely. For example, the cells that compose the nails or the hair are widely different from the cells that form the skin or muscular tissue, yet all cells are composed of protein, the substance 'of first importance'.

Enzymes, hormones, and internal secretions require certain combinations of amino acids or their derivatives. The hormone insulin, for example, requires seven specific amino acids for its synthesis by the pancreatic cells, according to L.F. Cooper in 'Nutrition in Health and Disease',

A limited amount of protein is stored in the liver in the form of amino acids, but in the absence of dietary protein these reserves do not last long. What happens is that body processes turn to the organs and muscles themselves when they are deprived of food protein and these are broken down to supply the necessary amino acids. This, of course, is highly undesirable and is something to be avoided at all times of life. The menopausal woman is just as likely to suffer as the growing teenager or the mature female.

Proteins Usually Skimped

Because protein foods are relatively expensive, they are most likely to be deficient in the diet. This applies particularly to the teenager, particularly where large families are compelled to exist on inadequate incomes.

The most concentrated and least expensive forms of protein are skim milk powder, wheatgerm, unprocessed cheese, and eggs. Even people who live on a restricted budget should strive to obtain adequate protein, without which their health must suffer.

The protein intake should not fall below 45g per day even for short periods.

Most women from the late-teens age group to the post-menopausal will, at some time in their lives, embark upon a weight-reducing programme. This is where they must be very conscious of their protein intake since a reduced calorie intake, which is what slimmers should aim for, is usually accompanied by less protein in the diet. They must keep at least 45g of protein per day in their calorie-controlled diets, and at the same time should take a good all-round multivitamin/multimineral supplement to supply the essential nutrients that a reduced food intake will not provide. Avoidance of excess body weight is to be desired throughout life, but we shall see how this applies specifically to the menopausal woman.

Weight Increase

Most women begin the menopause in an overweight condition, and one-third of women put on considerably more weight during the menopause.

The average woman suffers from 'low thyroid' or 'mild thyroid' deficiency; this deficiency may be due to a lack of iodine. The body activities become sluggish; the peristaltic action of the whole alimentary canal slows down, and constipation develops. Fewer calories are burned to produce energy, and the person thus affected becomes tired, lazy, has little endurance, and suffers from bad circulation and cold.

The addition of kelp to the diet (three tablets daily) usually works a transformation. The overweight woman should also take two B-complex and one vitamin C tablet before each meal. These vitamins (and the effect of the kelp tablet) help to promote enzymes which convert one's food into energy instead of into fat.

With regard to weight, it is interesting to recall that in the examination of two groups of women in an American sanitorium, the thin women and those of normal weight had a much easier passage through the menopause than the fat and overweight women.

Obesity puts an added strain on the entire human organism. It can lead to gall-bladder and other trouble. For women in middle life it may mean one or more of the following developments:

1. Increased strain on the heart mechanism.
2. High blood pressure.
3. Deterioration of muscular structure.
4. Prolapse of the bowel.
5. Backache.
6. Fallen arches.

Middle-aged spread does not always start during middle age. It often starts in the thirties and goes on increasing slowly so that it becomes noticeable only around the time of the menopause. As the woman grows older, her basal rate of metabolism decreases which means that she needs fewer calories. Unfortunately, her intake of food which gives rise to calories usually stays about the same and the inevitable consequence is that because calorie intake exceeds calorie use, weight increase follows. However, weight increase at the menopause has other causes too.

What happens is the swelling of the fingers and ankles occurs and these effects are due to retention of water in the tissues. These symptoms are often worse before periods or at the menopause. The simplest treatment is herbal diuretics, which can be as effective as diuretic drugs but which are without the side effects. A reduced salt intake may also help.

Distension of the gut due to its being blown up with wind is another feature of the menopause in many women. It can also happen in younger women before the periods or during the early months of pregnancy. Certain foods such as onions, pork and beans may make it worse. One way to tackle the problem is to eat the day's main meal at lunchtime instead of during the evening. There are many effective herbal preparations for this condition, although simple charcoal tablets often help.

There is no reason why a woman should lose her figure because of the onset of the menopause. She needs to control her calorie intake to achieve the ideal weight for her height. There are many tables relating weight to height, and the calorie content of foods can also be worked out from standard tables. Wholefood and health food diets are preferable to many other types of diet. They do not contain 'empty' calories and the concurrent intake of vitamins and minerals provided by these diets also helps in controlling weight. Sweets, chocolate, cream, cakes, biscuits, white bread, steamed puddings and alcohol all constitute calories out of proportion to their food value.

The muscles can be toned up and hence the figure is retained by using energy in the form of exercise. Move around more and faster, walk to work whenever possible and try to continue dancing and swimming. Remember that when you are overweight, the weight-bearing joints, i.e. the hips and knees, all begin to show signs of wear and tear and the consequences can include rheumatic disease. In addition, extra strain is put on the heart and lungs, so the benefits of avoiding excess weight during the menopause are substantial.

Excessive retention of body water is only one factor that is going to make the menopausal woman overweight. There is also the problem of surplus fat and, in some ways, this is more serious. No doctor can emphasize too stongly the dangers which derive from the accumulation of fatty tissue during and following the menopause. Not only does the female form lose its attractive lines, but internally, *where it is not seen*, its effect is most insidious.

Fat accumulates around the heart and impedes that most vital organ in its work. *One person in four dies of heart failure.*

The transverse colon, instead of lying horizontally across the body, sags sadly in the middle, causing constipation, and sometimes a complete blockage of the bowel. Indeed, every organ, and every physiological function, works under a serious handicap when embedded in surplus fatty tissue. Obesity is a most potent factor in ageing people much faster than their years, and cutting short the normal life span.

No wonder insurance companies, after long experience, take a dim view of the person whose organs are entombed in fat. Only diet along the lines laid down can meet the problem — diet and the *will* to follow it *consistently.* The foods that are fat-forming are the starchy and sugary foods, rather than the actual fatty foods.

The reward is not merely an easy passing through the menopause, but the preservation of one's youthful lines, a remarkable freedom from the current crop of human ailments, and positive increase in one's vitality and sense of well-being.

Exercise is an important supplement to diet in preserving one's figure and keeping organs in their right place. Exercise does not mean 'physical jerks'. It means a daily walk and such exercises as involve the graceful bending of the trunk to give tone to abdominal muscles in particular. Make a daily practice of contracting the abdominal muscles a dozen times a day.

Most housewifes obtain sufficient exercise in the daily performance of their 'chores', to satisfy requirements.

The Thyroid Gland

It is probable that all the endocrine glands have greater duties to perform to maintain the glandular balance once the ovarian glands cease to function.

A much greater strain is definitely put upon the thyroid gland at this time, and this is the chief reason why so many women develop signs of goitre after the menopause.

The raw material for the thyroid secretion is iodine. We only require a minute amount each day, but that infinitely small amount is of vital importance. The absence of adequate iodine (in our daily food) can cause not only an enlargement of the thyroid gland itself, but also may give rise to a number of minor ailments, including one or more of the following:

1. A lack of vitality.
2. Susceptibility to cold, particularly at the extremities.
3. 'Lifeless' hair and dandruff-inflicted scalp.
4. A slowing down of the peristaltic action of the bowel (regular contractions of the intestinal and bowel walls) and constipation.
5. Constant tiredness, a symptom felt by some women at the menopause.
6. Increase in weight.
7. A feeling of depression.
8. Lack of sex desire.

How to Remedy Thyroid Deficiency

Women who are in the habit of having regular seafood or taking kelp (powdered seaweed) should not suffer any of the symptoms of thyroid deficiency. This is *not* the signal, however, to indulge in plates of oysters or frequent meals of fish.

Oysters, while rich enough in iodine, are a grossly overrated food, and eating fish once a week provides as much of this type of protein as we require.

In most districts where the soil contains iodine, the most assured source of supply is to be found in the salad vegetables — the darker green leaves of lettuce, spinach, grated carrot and beetroot, parsley and celery.

But to be on the safe side about one's iodine supply, every woman who shows definite signs of thyroid deficiency should take one kelp tablet before each meal at the time of the menopause. Kelp tablets are made from concentrated seaweed and contain iodine and other minerals.

Tincture of iodine, which has an alcohol base, should not be taken as a substitute because it is a poison.

Incidentally, the vitamin B group (obtainable from B-complex vitamin tablets, wheatgerm and yeast) 'have a profound effect on the action of the thyroid gland', to quote from the famous nutritional authority Gayelord Hauser.

He points out that, as shown by the results of numerous experiments in which this effect was studied, the output of thyroxin (the hormone produced by the thyroid gland) was found to be decreased by 80 per cent when no B vitamins were included in the animal's diet.

Hauser concludes: 'These findings indicate that people suffering from symptoms of an underactive thyroid should increase both iodine and the vitamins of the B family in their diets.'

However, it is important to realize that an underactive thyroid may not necessarily be due to a lack of iodine in the diet. Sometimes adequate iodine is being supplied to the gland, but it has lost its ability to incorporate the mineral into the hormone, thyroxine. The usual reason is because the person has had part or all of their thyroid gland removed surgically. In such cases, there is no alternative to treatment with the hormone itself, and it is a relatively simple one involving taking tablets daily. Diagnosis of whether thyroid insufficiency is due to a lack of iodine or a lack of thyroxine is best left in the hands of the doctor who has at his disposal sophisticated tests to determine where the deficiency lies. This, however, does not detract from the usefulness of ensuring a good daily intake of iodine and this is best done by daily tablets of inexpensive kelp at the suggested dose.

The Value of Kelp
Kelp is gathered from the ocean, cleansed, dried, powdered and tableted. Weight for weight, it is the best source of mineral wealth of any food known to man. This is because it is not only a rich source of organic iodine, but is an amazing cornucopia of other essential minerals, lacking in the modern diet.

Dr J.W. Turrentine, eminent nutritional authority of the U.S. Department of Agriculture, has said: 'Of the fourteen elements essential to the proper metabolic functions of the human body, thirteen are known to be in kelp.... It should be made available for all people in all lands.'

Dr Sir William Arbuthnot Lane, famous English

medical authority, has written:

'In order to carry out its work, the thyroid gland must have iodine; the gland cannot create iodine. This element must come from *outside* the body.'

Kelp contains not only iodine, it also has useful traces of other elements necessary to health; namely iron, copper, calcium, phosphorus, potassium, sulphur, sodium, magnesium, manganese, chlorine, cobalt, iron, and barium.

There is evidence that the thyroid gland requires vitamins A, C, and B-complex as well as iodine, in order to function properly, and infections of the thyroid in laboratory animals have been produced by depriving them of these vitamins. Infections are produced more readily if the thyroid is already lacking in iodine.

A shortage of unsaturated fatty acids is also held to be a contributing factor in causing thyroid gland disorders and to overcome this, the use of lecithin or sunflower oil capsules is advisable, as both are excellent sources of unsaturated fatty acids.

The Importance of Calcium
Calcium performs so many important functions in the maintenance of health, that it may justly be designated the wonder mineral. One authority has said: 'Calcium is the prime instigator of vital activity.'

Yet, for all this, calcium is notoriously deficient in the modern diet, and particularly so in the diet of older people. Official U.S. figures state that probably 85 per cent of American people are short of calcium in their daily diet. Studies made in Toronto, Canada, revealed that 77 per cent of people who came for dental attention, suffered from lack of calcium. According to Prof. Sir

Stanton Hicks, eminent Australian authority on nutrition, the Australian diet, too, lacks calcium.

Calcium is the most abundant mineral in the body, mainly by virtue of its combination with phosphorus to form calcium phosphate, the main structural component of the skeleton and of the teeth. Bone is constantly being formed and dissolved and in the adult as much as 700mg of calcium enter and leave the bones in any one day. Calcium is also regularly excreted in the urine and swe... Such losses are independent of intake, so if not replaced, they will slowly deplete the body of its calcium reserves.

Two factors determine how much calcium is going to be absorbed into the body. The first is the quantity of the mineral in the food and the second is the amount of vitamin D taken with it. Calcium cannot be absorbed without vitamin D and incorporation into bone is also under the influence of this vitamin plus a hormone called parathyroid hormone. This is made by glands known as the parathyroids, located on each side of the neck adjacent to the thyroid gland. Hence, deficiency of calcium in adults (known as osteomalacia) can be caused either by a lack of calcium in the diet or by a lack of vitamin D which enables the mineral to be absorbed. The menopausal woman should therefore look to her intake of these essential nutrients.

The best sources of calcium are undoubtedly dairy products and canned fish. The latter are rich sources because of their content of soft edible bones which will supply both calcium and phosphorus. Canned sardines, for example, contain 156mg of calcium per ounce and canned salmon 26mg per ounce. Hard cheeses compare favourably with this (e.g. Cheddar contains 227mg and processed cheese contains 199mg per ounce), but cottage and cream cheeses contain much less at 17mg and 28mg per ounce respectively.

For the non-fish and non-dairy product eaters, bread (white), wheatgerm, soya flour, cabbage, watercress and dates provide 28mg, 24mg, 60mg, 16mg, 63mg and 17mg per ounce. All types of beans, broccoli, cauliflower and dried fruit provide meaningful amounts of calcium too. Wholemeal bread contains only 7mg per ounce because, unlike white bread, it does not contain added calcium. This does not, however, compensate for the overwhelming attributes of wholemeal bread. A pint of milk, incidentally contains 670mg of calcium.

The menopausal woman should aim at a diet that will supply at least 600mg of calcium daily and preferably 800mg. At the same time, she requires a daily intake of some 400 IU (10 micrograms) of vitamin D, and the richest sources of this vitamin are fish liver oils (cod, halibut etc.) and dairy products. It is also added by law to soft and hard margarines, so these represent an important source of vitamin D for the vegetarian. Vitamin D occurs naturally only in food products of animal origin; there is none in fruits, vegetables or seed and nut oils. Fortunately, however, the vitamin is produced in the skin in significant quantities, but only when the surface of the skin is exposed to sunlight. Hence, during the summer months, dietary intake of vitamin D becomes less important as long as the skin is exposed to the summer light. The vitamin is stored, so good exposure to the sun by the menopausal woman during the spring and summer months will ensure adequate reserves to satisfy her demands during the darker months.

Supplements of both calcium and vitamin D are

available to ensure the menopausal woman obtains her requirements without reference to those in her diet. The best absorbed calcium is that presented in the organic amino acid-chelated form, and is available as amino-chelated calcium, bonemeal and dolomite. The latter two preparations have the added advantage of supplying phosphorus and magnesium respectively.

Calcium's Enemies

It is essential that there be an acid medium to enable the body to utilize calcium. This means that the gastric juice should contain an adequate amount of hydrochloric acid, or calcium will remain insoluble and be lost to the body.

Antacid powders, carb. soda, and health salts neutralize the hydrochloric acid in the stomach, thus making the assimilation of calcium almost impossible and rendering the digestion of protein foods difficult. Excessive consumption of fatty foods prevents the proper assimilation of calcium. Conversely, if fat is excluded from the diet, the benefit from calcium is almost wholly lost.

Oxalic acid and phytic acid are two natural consituents of food that can react with calcium, forming an insoluble complex that renders the mineral unavailable for absorption. Foods that contain large amounts of oxalic acid, such as spinach and rhubarb, should be eaten sparingly, and chocolate and cocoa should not be eaten in excess for the same reason. Phytic acid occurs in grains, cereals and vegetables, but only when cereals are eaten in excess to produce an imbalanced diet does the phytic acid content contribute significantly to calcium immobilization.

Calcium is also lost to the body if there is a lack of

lecithin, if there is inadequate protein in the diet or if certain medicinal drugs are used for long periods. These include antacid medicines and the corticosteroids.

The symptoms of calcium deficiency may first show in the bone structure and include pains in the joints, brittleness of bones and bone aches upon exertion. Other functions are also affected.

Insufficiency of calcium results in many unpleasant symptoms. Calcium is not only required to maintain the health of the bone structure and teeth, but also the nerves. Adequate calcium helps the nerves to be steady and relaxed. A lack of it leads to tenseness, irritability, 'jumpiness', touchiness, uneasiness and insomnia.

Osteoporosis in the Menopause

When lost calcium from the bone is not replaced from the diet, a disease called osteoporosis results. The bones literally become honeycombed and brittle; the condition is very difficult to treat. This is because the basis of the problem is not just inefficient absorption of the calcium from the food, but an inability of the bone to accept calcium from the blood. Loss of calcium from the bone which we have seen is a constant feature of its metabolism, occurs more frequently in women, particularly at the time of the menopause. No one is quite certain why this is so, but it appears that lack of production of oestrogen is an important factor. This hormone somehow enables women to use more of the calcium in their food.

Osteoporosis is a progressive thinning of the bones that can leave the skeleton too brittle to withstand even minimal stress. Indeed, the bones of the spine can become so papery that they collapse; five vertebrae may fill the space occupied by three, causing a protuberance known as 'dowager's hump'. The result is a marked stoop.

The condition is improved by ensuring the woman walks upright and sits straight in a high-backed chair. Carrying heavy loads should be avoided to prevent strain on the spine. It is important to keep active by walking, swimming and dancing, because calcium leaks away from the bones while you rest.

Simple increase of dietary calcium may not be sufficient on its own to treat osteoporosis once this has started, but there is evidence that the important period in which to ensure adequate calcium intake is early and middle life. The later development of osteoporosis may then be prevented. Although the disease is difficult to treat, there are reports that calcium supplements have induced calcium retention and relieved symptoms, indicating that while absorption may not increase, this treatment cuts down calcium loss.

The Heart

When it is realized that one person in four dies of heart disease, or heart failure, it is not surprising that the age of the menopause will find most hearts somewhat affected. When we consider, further, that the menopause is often characterized by congestions of blood and rushes of blood to the head, it is not to be wondered that the heart will show some abnormal or subnormal symptoms during this period.

The most general complaint that women have during the menopause, so far as the heart is concerned, is palpitation or a racing pulse, or both. The condition may come on suddenly — sometimes in the night — and it may pass as quickly as it came. The symptom frightens many women, and quite without reason, since these palpitations are due more to a general nervous condition. They are not due — in the great majority of cases — to organic heart weakness.

The most sensible thing that any woman can do about them is to follow the diet recommended for the menopause as closely as possible, have plenty of rest, and refrain from worrying. The diet recommended will do much to repair any real damage to the heart that may have been done over the years.

There is now no doubt that a woman is more likely to develop a coronary after the menopause than before it, although she is still at less risk of this than a man of comparable age. One simple way to decrease the chances of a coronary is to stop smoking. The exercise regime mentioned above under weight increase should also benefit the heart. Partial replacement of butter and lard by corn or maize oil in cooking and by polyunsaturated soft margarine in cooking and eating will contribute to a healthy heart. Shop more at the greengrocer and fishmonger and health food shop instead of at the butcher and confectioner and supermarket. Simple enjoyment of life and reduction of stress will increase relaxation and cut down the mental contribution to heart disease.

4

Treatment of the Menopause

Natural treatments of the symptoms of the menopause using vitamins, minerals and herbs are now available. To these must be added the purely medicinal treatment of Hormone Replacement Therapy (HRT) which is essentially an attempt to replace those hormones which are no longer being produced by the woman herself. These hormones may be the naturally occurring ones or the synthetic variety. However, preparation for the menopause should be in the hands of the woman herself and her diet will play an important part in this.

(i) How to Prepare for the Menopause
For all women who would have an easy menopause, who desire to pass through the change of life with the minimum of upset to their health and peace of mind, there is one golden rule: *The better your general health before the menopause the easier you will pass through.* In other words, *make sure of your health* and the menopause will take care of itself.

How can a high standard of good health be achieved? A small percentage of women seem to enjoy good health, no matter what they do or what they eat. But the average woman finds that to enjoy first-class health she has to make an *objective* attempt to get it. That is to say, good health is not just given most women on a platter. It cannot be bought, like cosmetics. It can only be acquired by the consistent and persistent application of intelligence to selecting and eating health-giving foods and avoiding the foods which, though perhaps tempting to the palate, are distastrous to the health.

Most authorities are agreed that *sound nutrition* is the best armour against the crop of troubles lying in wait for every woman at the menopause and after. Sound nutrition may be summarized as follows:

1. Meals must be very simple, though quite adequate in fundamentals. Complex mixtures are out!

2. Foods must be *vital*. That is to say, one must eat *live* foods and eschew all *devitalized* foods.

The live foods are the uncooked fruits and salad vegetables, or vegetables lightly steamed, raw milk, butter, wheatgerm, nuts and raisins, cheese, eggs, and lightly grilled meat or fish.

The devitalized foods are white flour products, sugar, dried foods, breakfast grains that are blown out with steam and toasted to death, tea and coffee, jam, pastry, biscuits, confectionery, sausage meats and all those picturesque but devitalized foodstuffs of the delicatessen.

Crops grown on sick soils *are sick crops,* no matter how good they look. Soils treated with superphosphates lack the humus needed to feed the plant roots. Superphosphates are made of phosphates, treated with sulphuric acid, and it is this acid which destroys the earthworm population and the beneficent soil bacteria.

Let us consider now the vegetables grown for city populations. These are usually 'forced' with the assistance of chemical fertilizers and such vegetables, having to pass through many hands; namely, grower, trucker, market-middleman, and then retailer, are usually stale and lacking in vitamins by the time they reach the housewife.

Fruits for the consumption of city dwellers, are invariably picked green, and ripened artificially. Sometimes they are ripened chemically and coloured with dyes.

Fruit trees are sprayed with poisonous compounds to keep down pests. Much of this spray falls on to the ground, to kill earthworms and soil bacteria and then to be absorbed by the tree roots and incorporated in the sap which feeds the fruit.

Our advice to those with back gardens is to make compost heaps and to grow as much of their own fruit and vegetables as possible.

Ideal Diet for the Menopause

The foregoing provides a sound outline for the woman who desires to get through the menopause with the minimum of disturbance and the maximum of good health.

Let us now translate those principles into a diet chart, so that every woman will clearly understand what she must do and why.

Pre-breakfast

If you have been in the habit of having an early morning cup of tea, you will find it hard to break. It is not the best way, however, to break your fast. So try very hard to cultivate the practice of having a glass of diluted orange juice first thing.

If you can't get orange juice, use pineapple juice or tomato juice, tinned or fresh, or diluted lemon juice. Failing any of these juices, take one 250mg vitamin C tablet.

Breakfast

Breakfast should be a simple meal composed of a balance of protein, complex carbohydrates, vegetable oils and dietary fibre. Muesli is preferred to refined cereals because its content of grains and nuts will provide protein, vegetable oils and dietary fibre. The dried fruit is an excellent source of energy, minerals and fruit fibre. The protein of muesli can be supplemented with that of eggs which, preferably, should be boiled or scrambled. Fried eggs should be limited and cooked only in vegetable oils. Meats, including bacon, should also be limited to no more than once per week because of the saturated fat content and high salt content of these foods. Wholemeal bread is preferred to the devitalized white variety.

But there is one vital food which, if you have not already added it to your breakfast, you simply must do so now. That food is wheatgerm. Wheatgerm is the germ of the wheat, and is removed in the refining of flour.

Nutritional science has learned in recent years that wheatgerm is a 'valuable food', containing 8 B vitamins, 6 essential minerals, and 12 amino acids. (Amino acids are the valuable cell-building elements we get from protein foods.)

The B vitamins are absolutely necessary for sound nerves and the appalling amount of neuroticism and 'nerves' in the general public of this era is in no small measure due to the refining of flour and the removal of the germ of the wheat.

The practice in the past has been to feed the wheatgerm to pigs, who thrive on it. The poor humans, who have been starved of it, have developed a whole crop of ailments due to the lack of this precious substance, including nervous disorders, constipation and anaemia.

Few people suffer any more from nerves, constipation and anaemia once wheatgerm has taken the place of stodgy, starchy, constipating porridge meals at breakfast. Buy a good brand of wheatgerm—not in bulk— and have it with milk (hot in winter) or with grated apple, or with stewed apricots, prunes, stewed apple, or raisins.

Two or three dessertspoonsful of wheatgerm, with milk and fruit (raw or stewed) constitutes an ample breakfast for any woman.

Before breakfast take 1 B$_1$ (10mg), 1 B complex, 1 kelp, 2 calcium tablets and 1 50mg vitamin E tablet (or capsule), all together and after breakfast 2 vitamin A and D capsules (cod liver oil).

Mid-morning
Having held off tea for so long, you will find an added enjoyment in a cup now. But note two things: strong tea is an enemy, though a subtle one, of good health. I suggest that it is not too late at 40 to gradually accustom yourself to weaker tea or a herbal tea.

The second point is that sugar is even worse than tea. Both are common causes of acidity—the beginning of all ill health—but sugar is the greater offender because, not only is it acid-forming, but it neutralizes the calcium in the bloodstream. In other words, refined sugar robs you of your calcium, which is essential for sound bones, sound teeth and *sound nerves*.

So away with the sugar bowl. If you must sweeten your tea, use honey. Better still, by taking less and less sugar, you can lose your 'sweet tooth' altogether over a period of six months.

Yes, a slice of toast is permitted at morning tea! Try it with butter and yeast extract.

Lunch

The ideal lunch is one of the following:

1. Two apples and 3oz of Cheddar cheese.
2. A large salad with egg, or cheese.
3. Fruit and milk.

If you had milk with your wheatgerm you won't want much now. Never have more than 1 pint of milk a day. Too much milk is mucus-forming.

With regard to No. 1: The apple provides a perfect digestive acid for the cheese and, eaten in this way, cheese does not constipate.

Intelligence needs to be used for the selection of a fruit lunch. The juices of apples and pears are incompatible. Bananas belong to the starch, or carbohydrate, family. Sliced on a salad, or in a fruit salad, they possess a high energizing value. Apples, or grapes, or peaches, or pawpaws, eaten separately, are the ideal lunch fruit.

Before lunch, the ideal diet requires 1 B_1 (10mg), 1 B-complex, 1 kelp, 2 calcium tablets. After lunch take 2 vitamin A and D capsules (cod liver oil).

Afternoon

Nutritional science strongly recommends fruit juices or

fruit in preference to tea and cakes. Rich cakes are a potential cause of that ugly, overweight condition that every self-respecting woman who wants to hold her self-regard and the regard of her husband, should make a strong effort to avoid.

The same reasoning applies to most forms of confectionery. They are acid-forming, calcium-robbing, fat-producing products, and the wise woman will permit herself to indulge in sweet-eating on occasions too rare to matter.

A cup of weak tea and a thin slice of wholemeal bread and butter, if you must have afternoon tea.

The Evening Meal

If you haven't had a salad for lunch, make sure of having it at night. The salad, from the point of view of nutrition, is the ideal meal. A proper salad supplies most of the mineral elements needed by the body.

Remarkably few families know what a real, honest-to-goodness salad is. Here's the salad we like best:

Finely shredded *green* lettuce leaves, parsley and a little mint. Grate carrot, beetroot and apple. Mix the lot in a bowl and serve on plates with slices of ripe sugar bananas and a pear or pineapple.

That is a fruit salad and a large plate of it is designed to satisfy any appetite. If something else is wanted, follow it with a little home-made ice cream (sweetened with honey); or grapes or peaches.

Another simpler type of salad consists of sliced banana and parsley rolled in lettuce leaves and eaten by hand. Still another type of salad consists of lettuce, carrot, tomatoes, shredded cabbage, celery, and watercress. In this case, omit the fruit and the beetroot. This type of salad can be eaten with a slice of cold meat, ham, cheese, cream cheese, sliced eggs, sardines, cold fish, etc. Dessert should consist of fruit only, but not bananas.

Even on the coldest winter's night a salad can be enjoyed, provided it is preceded by a plate of hot soup—not soup cooked to death in the old, traditional stock pot, but grated vegetables boiled for ten minutes. Alternatively, tomato *purée*.

Salad dressings are a matter of taste. A little thin cream is ideal—if you can get it—for the first type of salad. A little olive oil and lemon juice, or lemon juice only, for the third type of salad, garnished with meat, cheese, eggs, fish, etc.

If you have acquired a taste for kelp you may not need any additional iodine in the form of kelp tablets.

As to meat, the ideal diet insists that it be used not more than once daily. Cheese is a more valuable protein.

If you have no appetite for a meal, don't eat. Alternatively, have an apple, or a bunch of grapes, or a fruit drink. A glass of orange juice has 300 calories of energy in it—which is quite a meal.

If you have been invited out and eaten unwisely, forego the next meal or two altogether, or be content with a fruit drink. The art of eating wisely is an *intelligent simplicity;* working always towards balance, but including the fundamental vitamins.

Before the evening meal, take 1 B_1 (10mg), 1 B-complex, 1 kelp, 2 calcium tablets and 1 vitamin E tablet (50mg) or capsule and after the meal take 2 vitamin A and D capsules.

The supplementary vitamins are of vital importance to a woman's health during and after the change of life.

And, incidentally, they cost no more than the average woman spends on cigarettes.

The traditional supper is taboo; better to be content with a diluted fruit drink. Better still, cultivate the habit of taking a teaspoonful of pasteurized yeast, mixed with a teaspoonful of skim milk powder in a glass of water, and sweetened with honey. Alternatively, take a couple of teaspoonsful of molasses—rich in iron and other minerals, and a natural laxative.

(ii) How Ginseng May Help
Ginseng is a herb root that has been used by the people of the Far East for at least 3000 years as a universal tonic, revitalizer, stimulant and all-round medicine. It is, however, only in the last ten years or so that research doctors and scientists have begun to understand why ginseng has these beneficial properties. The root contains a number of substances that have the ability to control hormone levels in the body. They are not in themselves hormones, but their chemical structure is not unlike that of the sex hormones and the anti-stress hormones. Oestrogens in the female and testosterone in the male are themselves normally under the control of other hormones, both in the amount produced and in their time of production. It appears that the substances in ginseng have similar properties and in their own way regulate the hormones required for body functions.

Since the menopause is characterized by a reduction in the production of oestrogens by the female ovaries, it would seem to be a logical step to stimulate the synthesis of these sex hormones to allow a more gradual cessation of their secretion. Clinical trials have now been carried out to test the use of ginseng in the menopause, and the results are highly encouraging.

In one German study, 72 women were tested with ginseng and vitamins and a further 72 received a placebo (i.e. tablets that look like ginseng and vitamins, but were in fact composed simply of sugar). Symptoms such as hot flushes, night sweating, nervous tension, headaches and palpitations disappeared completely in 43 of the 72 women receiving ginseng and vitamins. At the same time, mild depression, insomnia and sexual problems all responded favourably to the herb. Only 14 of those receiving the placebo treatment could claim similar benefits. The investigating doctor was a gynaecologist who stated that the ginseng and vitamins should be taken by women at an early stage on a purely preventative basis in order to increase and maintain their resistance capacity and to prevent possible menopausal disorders. Regular treatment will avoid the need for hormones.

Ginseng should be taken daily at a level of 600mg or 1200mg of whole root extract or a suitable comparative extract. The vitamins needed are some two to three times the minimum daily requirements and would be supplied by any good multivitamin preparation containing all the vitamins.

Another comprehensive trial was reported in 1977 from Kawasaki City Hospital in Japan. Patients suffering from menopausal disorders were divided into three groups:
1) those where chief complaints were excessive perspiration, hot flushes, headache, stiff shoulder, palpitations, fatigue, loss of appetite, apprehension and reduced sexual desire;
2) those whose symptoms were apprehension, sleeplessness, irritation, moodiness, palpitations, stiff neck,

reduced sexual desire. (These were classed as neurotic or depressed types.);

3) those who had received hysterectomy with chief complaints of perspiration, hot flushes, headache, stiff shoulder, fatigue, irritation, apprehension, sleeplessness and a sense of loss of femininity.

All of these received one capsule containing 200mg of ginseng root powder plus a concentrated ginseng liquid extract equivalent to 370mg of ginseng (taken in two doses of 20ml each, once morning and once evening). Their total intake was thus almost 600mg of ginseng per day. Treatment lasted from four to six weeks.

The response to ginseng was most gratifying: 82.4 per cent of group 1; 66.7 per cent of group 2 and 88.9 per cent of group 3 showed some beneficial effect. Most were a marked or good effect, but the total response averaged 81.3 per cent. Hence, four out of five women experiencing problems of the menopause can expect some benefit by simply taking 600mg of the root powder daily.

Other herbs have been used successfully in treating the symptoms of the menopause. For example, *Senecio vulgaris,* also known as life-root plant, is a uterine tonic which specifically helps the uterus to relax. It is beneficial also to the ovaries and the fallopian tubes. The root of the Mexican wild yam, *Dioscora villosa,* contains a substance not unlike those of ginseng which appears to have a regulating role on oestrogen production. It also relaxes the nervous system and so helps in the mental symptoms associated with the menopause.

Helonias dioica is a summer-flowering herbaceous plant common in the United States. It is an ovarian stimulant. When combined with feverfew, yarrow and yellow dock, it is specifically recommended for hot flushes since these herbs have a normalizing effect upon the blood circulation.

Three herbs that can benefit the nervous problems associated with the menopause are *Passiflora incarnata,* Valerian and *Cypripedium pubescens* (Lady's slipper). Motherwort *(Leonurus cardiaca)* is a heart tonic and is helpful in dealing with the heart irregularities that often accompany the menopause. The most widely used herb in Britain, however, is Golden Seal *(Hydrastis).* It has specific actions on the blood supply of the uterus and is sometimes combined with Birthroot (*Trillium*) in treating the symptoms of the menopause, including depression.

(iii) Vitamin E
The Shute Foundation for Medical Research has published much valuable data on the great benefits experienced by women who used vitamin E, in moderate dosages of 50 to 100 mg daily, during the menopause.

We quote from research documents published by the Shute Foundation:

'Oestrogens often give substantial relief from flushes and headache, and may relieve vulvo-vaginal pruritus (itching or irritation) or early kraurosis (a progressive shrivelling of the skin which affects the sex organ).

'But too many women achieve this at the price of vaginal bleeding, and this makes one apprehensive of genital malignancy.

'In many patients even small doses of oestrogenic substance are open to this objection.

'Now alpha tocopherol (vitamin E) decreases the intensity and frequency of hot flushes, although not so completely as do the oestrogens, and it never provokes vaginal bleeding, which is a major advantage.

'It often relieves the characteristic headache of the menopause. All this is accomplished on daily dosages of 50 to 100 milligrams, which must be maintained for many months, of course.

'But the most dramatic results it achieves are in pruritus vulvae or in kraurosis. There it is much superior to oestrogens, which often make these patients much worse.'

But in these severe itching irritations that torment so many women after the menopause, the dosage of vitamin E is higher, viz., up to 300 mg daily.

Dr Stella H. Sikkema, writing in the *Rocky Mountains Medical Journal* reviews 365 cases of women with severe menopausal symptoms being treated only with vitamin E. Two out of every three were greatly relieved.

Dr N. R. Kavinoky (U.S.A.) gave 100mg of vitamin E daily to 79 menopause patients. Flushes were greatly relieved in 76 per cent, sweats in 78 per cent, headache in 67 per cent, palpitations in 82 per cent, and breathlessness in 75 per cent.

Vitamin E improves the whole circulatory mechanism, strengthens the heart muscle, and benefits the general health at the most critical period of a woman's life, and saves her from deteriorating into the lower level of health and semi-sickness suffered by untold thousands of women during the menopause.

In a report of the value of vitamin E in the menopause, Dr C. J. Cristy (in the *American Journal of Gynaecology*) states that he gave this vitamin to a group of 25 patients with ages ranging from 22 to 55 years. No patient was treated who did not complain of severe symptoms. The amount taken varied from 10 to 30mg a day, depending upon the degree of severity of symptoms, over a period of from one to six weeks. Seven of the 25 patients reported complete relief, and sixteen reported great relief.

The use of vitamin E in the menopause has been actively studied by Dr Henry A. Gozan of New York. In the *New York State Journal of Medicine* he reported that oral vitamin E, taken at the rate of 100 IU three times per day over a three monthly period, helped relieve the hot flushes, the headaches and the nervous tension associated with the menopause. There was success in easing and eliminating these distressing symptoms in 59 out of 66 patients treated in this way.

According to the Shute Institute, vitamin E exerts its action in females by normalizing the blood levels of the female sex hormone. It dilates the blood vessels, at the same time ensuring a good supply of blood to the uterus. It also has the ability to improve the heat-regulating capacity of the body, which is why it helps in the excessive sweating that is often a feature of the menopause. Treatment with vitamin E during the menopause brings about a smoother transition to decreased production of oestrogen by the ovaries, and so avoids many of the problems induced by sudden cessation of the hormone flow.

(iv) Vitamin B_6

Healthy functioning of the brain and the nervous system depends upon the efficient production and eventual disposal of certain chemical substances. One of these is called serotonin, and when this is not secreted in the brain and nerve endings, a mild depression will often result. The control of mood is dependent on brain concentration of serotonin. Serotonin is synthesized in the body from a food constituent called L-tryptophan, and the controlling factor in this is vitamin B_6. Hence, a vitamin B_6 deficiency manifests itself first as a mild mental upset.

A woman approaching the menopause is quite likely to be deficient in vitamin B_6. There are many reasons for this. She may have been using the contraceptive pill for some years and this is known to induce a deficiency of the vitamin in some women. Alternatively, it can increase her requirements for B_6 to levels that she will not obtain even from a good diet. Some women appear to have an increased requirement of the vitamin anyway, even if not taking the Pill, and if suitable intakes are lacking, they are likely to suffer some of the symptoms loosely described as pre-menstrual tension (PMT).

Many drugs will have an adverse effect upon the vitamin B_6 status of a female, so if she is on certain medical treatments for a long time she will suffer a B_6 deficiency. Smoking tobacco and drinking alcohol are two social habits that contribute to a reduction of B_6 levels in the body.

It is therefore quite possible that at the menopause the vitamin B_6 status of the female is low. It is not unusual for a woman who suffers from pre-menstrual tension during her child-bearing years to have difficulties also at the menopause. There is a very good chance that her mental symptoms associated with PMT will clear up by simply taking a supplement of vitamin B_6. Similarly, when comparable mental upsets appear at the menopause, vitamin B_6 can often help.

The usual supplementary regime in PMT is 50 to 100mg of vitamin B_6 daily. This quantity may also help during the menopause—there is little point in taking more. If this treatment helps to relieve some of the menopausal symptoms, it can safely be taken on a daily basis for the duration of the condition. Of course, a healthy vitamin B_6 status before the menopause may help the woman to sail through this period of her life. Even at the post-menopausal stage, vitamin B_6 is often helpful.

(v) Hormone Replacement Therapy (HRT)

Although Hormone Replacement Therapy cannot be carried out by an individual for self-treatment, it is often the final resort of the desperate woman suffering the symptoms of the menopause. The rationale appears to be simple and logical. If the symptoms are due to lack of female hormones, replace them with the natural or synthetic variety. HRT finds a place where cessation of hormone production is abrupt or irregular. It is an attempt to smooth out and make gradual the inevitable reduction in hormone levels.

HRT is mainly useful in treating hot flushes and sweating when these are excessive. It also helps to lubricate the vagina by stimulating the flow of natural mucosal juices. There is little evidence that the treatment helps the depression and tiredness of the menopause and vitamin B_6 is more likely to help relieve these symptoms. Hopes that HRT will make a menopausal woman look more youthful are not always realized, but there is no doubt that some do look younger and prettier after treatment.

If the HRT is a combined cyclical preparation of oestrogen and progesterone hormones, it is quite possible for the woman to continue with her 'periods'. These may not be regular, but they can occur. It does not mean that she is still fertile since the hormones will not cause her to produce egg cells. If two years have elapsed after the last natural period before HRT is started, the woman is well past the egg-producing stage, and it is impossible for her to become pregnant. However, it is important to remember that menopausal oestrogen preparations are weaker than the Pill and are not efficient contraceptives. Other methods must therefore be used during the early part of the therapy, but the woman must be guided by her doctor.

Some advantages are conferred by the use of HRT. There is clinical evidence that HRT in post-menopausal women may protect against heart disease. The big benefit, however, appears to be in the treatment of osteoporosis when this is associated with the condition. HRT normalizes the uptake of calcium by the bone to replace that lost by natural exchange. Even temporary hormone replacement after the menopause will have a lasting beneficial effect upon the bones. This corresponds to the reduced rate of fractures reported in women who had received oestrogens for some years after the menopause, according to a *Lancet* report in February 1981.

Recent reports from the Mayo Clinic in Rochester, U.S.A. have suggested an alternative to HRT in treating the osteoporosis of the menopause. In a 12-year study, Dr B. Lawrence Riggs and his team have treated women with large doses of sodium fluoride combined with calcium. These minerals stimulate bone-forming cells to produce new bone faster than the old bone is broken down. Hence, fluoride and calcium are able to reverse the process, giving rise to osteoporosis. Preliminary results are encouraging, but the treatment is still in the early stages. If confirmed, such therapy would be expected to be safer than HRT.

HRT is not without its dangers, and often these must be weighed against its advantages. There is evidence that it may be associated with cancer of the womb, and some preparations cause changes in the blood clotting mechanisms. Obviously, HRT must be carried out under medical supervision since constant monitoring of the woman's reactions to it is essential. There is also the possibility of regular D and C (dilation and curettage) while on the treatment.

HRT is not suitable for those where there is a family history of cancer of the breast, uterus or ovaries, angina, high blood pressure, coronary thrombosis, deep vein thrombosis, diabetes, kidney or liver disease. There must therefore be a significant proportion of women who are unable to receive HRT. For these and many others the natural treatments and dietary suggestions described in this book must represent the first line of therapy during the period leading up to and including the menopause.

Index